LEGENDS OF THE NFL

By Tyler Blue

Abbeville Kids
An Imprint of Abbeville Press
New York London

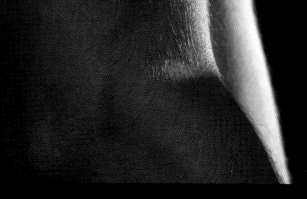

Please note: This book has not been authorized by the NFL.

Project editor: Lauren Orthey
Copy editor: Ashley Benning
Design: Ada Rodriguez
Production director: Louise Kurtz

PHOTOGRAPHY CREDITS

Adobe Stock: front cover background (103tnn), pp. 2–3 (Africa Studio), pp. 4–5 (.shock)

Alamy: front cover right (Zuma Press, Inc.), p. 7 (Zuma Press, Inc./Dan Anderson), p. 9 and front cover center (Archive PL), p. 13 (VTR), p. 15 (Zuma Press, Inc.), p. 17 (PA Images/Andrew Matthews), p. 21 (Zuma Press, Inc.), p. 25 (Rich Kane Photography), p. 27 (Zuma Press, Inc.), p. 29 (PCN Photography/PCN Black), p. 33 (PCN Photography/PCN Black), p. 35 and back cover top (UPI/Bruce Kluckhohn), p. 39 (UPI), p. 41 (Jonathan Kirn), p. 43 and back cover center (UPI), p. 45 (Zuma Press, Inc.), p. 47 (Rich Kane Photography), p. 49 (Rich Kane Photography), p. 51 (Rich Kane Photography), p. 53 (Zuma Press, Inc.), p. 57 (Zuma Press, Inc.), p. 59 and front cover left (Zuma Press, Inc.), p. 61 (Zuma Press, Inc.)

Icon Sportswire: p. 11 (Cliff Welch), p. 23 (Owen C. Shaw), p. 31 (Cliff Welch), p. 37 (Cliff Welch)

Library of Congress: pp. 62–63 (Carol M. Highsmith)

Wikimedia Commons: p. 19, p. 55, and back cover bottom (Malcolm W. Emmons)

First edition
10 9 8 7 6 5 4 3 2 1

ISBN 978-0-7892-1483-6

Library of Congress Cataloging-in-Publication Data available upon request

For bulk and premium sales and for text adoption procedures, write to Customer Service Manager, Abbeville Press, 655 Third Avenue, New York, NY 10017, or call 1-800-Artbook.

Visit Abbeville Kids online at **www.abbevillefamily.com**.

CONTENTS

Tom Brady

New England Patriots owner Bob Kraft vividly remembers meeting the 199th player selected in the 2000 NFL draft. The rookie quarterback, who was the seventh signal-caller taken that year, looked Kraft right in the eyes and said, "I'm the best decision this organization has ever made."

Over the course of his 23-year career that ended in 2022, Tom Brady played in 10 Super Bowls and won seven of them—more than any other player in NFL history. He was a 15-time Pro Bowler and holds just about every record a quarterback can have, including most career passing yards (89,214), most career passing touchdowns (649), and most career wins by a quarterback (251). So it is easy to forget that the story of Brady is, above all, the tale of an underdog.

For much of his early life, Tom was overshadowed. Born on August 3, 1977, in San Mateo, California, he was the little brother to three very athletic and very accomplished sisters. His oldest sister Maureen was an All-American softball pitcher at Fresno State; Julie played soccer at St. Mary's College of California; and Nancy earned a softball scholarship to the University of California at Berkeley.

Of course, young Tom wasn't exactly a slouch. At Junipero Serra High School, he gained a reputation for being an extremely hard worker. He actually developed the football team's workout and training schedule. He excelled both on the gridiron and the baseball diamond. In fact, Major League Baseball's Montreal Expos chose him in the 18th round of the 1995 draft. Instead, Tom decided to play football at the University of Michigan.

At Michigan, Brady was once again overshadowed, first by quarterback Brian Griese, the son of NFL Hall of Fame quarterback Bob Griese. Brian led the Wolverines to a national championship in 1997. After Griese graduated, Brady had to contend with hotshot quarterback recruit Drew Henson, whom many considered a can't-miss superstar. Brady began his senior year by splitting time with Henson. But Brady consistently outplayed his rival and by year's end was the sole starter.

Even so, NFL scouts pegged Brady more as a solid backup than a future Hall of Famer. And Brady began his career as the Patriots' No. 2 quarterback behind Drew Bledsoe. That all changed on September 23, 2001, in a home game against the New York Jets. With 5:03 left, Jets linebacker Mo Lewis made perhaps the most consequential tackle in NFL history, slamming into Bledsoe along the right sideline. Bledsoe sustained a serious injury, and Brady got an opening.

Though he didn't put up big numbers, Brady kept racking up wins. New England went 11–3 in the games Brady started, and the Patriots qualified for the playoffs. Brady kept winning, leading New England to the franchise's first NFL championship against the heavily favored St. Louis Rams in Super Bowl XXXVI. Brady was named game MVP. That offseason, the Patriots traded Bledsoe, making it official: New England was Tom Brady's team.

New England would win five more Super Bowls during the Brady era, which ended following the 2019 season when Brady signed with the Tampa Bay Buccaneers. He won his seventh championship in his first year with Tampa. And that's how an underdog becomes the GOAT.

Position: **Quarterback**
Hometown: **San Mateo, CA**
Born: **Aug. 3, 1977**
Height: **6'4"**
Weight: **225 lbs.**
Teams: **New England Patriots (2000–2019), Tampa Bay Buccaneers (2020–22)**
Career Passing Yards: **89,214**

Jim Brown

It took Cleveland Browns running back Jim Brown just nine seasons to completely rewrite the NFL record books. When he retired before the 1966 season at age 30–a decision that shocked everyone, as he was still very much in his prime–nobody had rushed for more yards (12,312), run for more touchdowns (106), or scored more total touchdowns (126).

Additionally, Brown, who never missed a game, led the league in rushing eight times and made the Pro Bowl in each of his nine seasons. Brown averaged 104.3 rushing yards per game, making him still the only player in NFL history to run for more than 100 yards per game in his career. And this was all while playing in an era when defenses prioritized stopping the run over stopping the pass.

In short, few players have dominated the NFL like Jim Brown.

James Nathaniel Brown was born on St. Simons Island, Georgia, on February 17, 1936. His father, a professional boxer, abandoned the family when Jim was just a couple of weeks old. Not long afterward, Jim's mother took a job as a maid on Long Island. Jim stayed behind and was raised by his great-grandmother. His first school was a segregated two-room shack.

When Jim's mother finally sent for him, Jim was eight and they hadn't seen each other for six years. Jim acclimated well to his new environment. At Manhasset High School, he lettered in football, basketball, baseball, lacrosse, and track. During his senior year, he averaged a ridiculous 14.9 yards per carry as a running back as well as 38 points per game on the hardwood. Off the field, Jim's peers elected him chief justice of the high school court, and he was a member of the honor society for scholastic achievement.

Brown decided to lend his robust athletic talents to Syracuse University. As a sophomore, he led the football team in rushing, averaged 15 points per game for the basketball team, and lettered in track. His senior year, he was a first-team All-American in both football and lacrosse. He was such a dominant lacrosse player that he was later voted into that sport's Hall of Fame.

But football was Brown's future. Cleveland chose him with the sixth pick of the 1957 NFL draft. Brown's combination of size, power, and speed proved overwhelming. He won Rookie of the Year after leading the league with 942 yards. "As a pure runner, Jim stands alone," Brown's coach Paul Brown said.

He certainly did. Brown led the league in rushing his first five years and then again in his final three seasons. He helped the Browns win an NFL championship in 1964. In 1965, which would become his final season, Brown rushed for 1,544 yards, scored a total of 21 touchdowns, and was named league MVP.

Then, while at the top of his game, Brown suddenly called it quits prior to the 1966 season. He had a role in the Hollywood film *The Dirty Dozen* and decided to concentrate his time on his movie career and furthering race relations. He would go on to appear in over 30 movies.

Brown was inducted into the Pro Football Hall of Fame in 1971. He died peacefully in his sleep on May 18, 2023, at the age of 87.

Position: **Running Back**
Hometown: **St. Simons Island, GA**
Born: **Feb. 17, 1936**
Died: **May 18, 2023**
Height: **6'2"**
Weight: **232 lbs.**
Team: **Cleveland Browns (1957–65)**
Career Rushing Yards Per Game: **104.3**

Dick Butkus

As the youngest of nine children born to a blue-collar family of Lithuanian descent in the Fernwood neighborhood on the South Side of Chicago, Richard Marvin "Dick" Butkus learned from an early age how to compete and work for what he wanted. And by the time he was in fifth grade, Butkus already knew that, more than anything else in the world, he wanted to play professional football.

From that point on, just about every decision the future Chicago Bears Hall of Fame middle linebacker made was in pursuit of his professional ambitions. To strengthen his legs, he would push a car up and down the street. To simulate avoiding blockers, he would sprint at trees before dodging them at the last second. He even chose to travel several more miles than necessary to attend Chicago Vocation High School because the football program was run by a former Notre Dame player named Bernie O'Brien.

It was at CVHS that Dick first made a name for himself as a fierce defender, while developing an uncanny ability to strip the ball from runners when making a tackle. Butkus carried this skill with him his entire career. In fact, when he retired from football following the NFL 1973 season, no player in league history had more fumble recoveries than Butkus's 25.

When the time came for the athlete to choose a college, he had to decide between the Fighting Irish of Notre Dame and the Fighting Illini of the University of Illinois. Though just a teenager, he was already contemplating marrying his high school sweetheart Helen Essenberg, and he heard the Irish frowned on married players. So he stayed in state and committed to Illinois. While he was there, Helen and Dick did indeed marry, in 1963, and were together until his death on October 5, 2023.

Butkus led the Illini to a Rose Bowl victory in 1963, and in 1964 he came in third place in the Heisman Trophy voting–the highest defensive vote getter at the time. The Bears selected him as the third overall pick of the 1965 NFL draft. The 6'3", 245-pound wrecking ball made his mark right from the get-go, recording 11 solo tackles in his first professional game on his way to being selected to the Pro Bowl and being named a first-team All-Pro.

An absolute terror sideline to sideline, there was no player as intimidating and feared as Butkus, who viewed his opponents as enemies. Regarding facing Butkus, former Green Bay Packers running back MacArthur Lane once said, "If I had a choice, I'd sooner go one-on-one with a grizzly bear."

Knee injuries limited Butkus to just nine seasons, but he made the Pro Bowl in eight of those years, and he was a first-team All-Pro in five of them. He was elected to the Hall of Fame in 1979, the first year he was eligible. In a further testament to his lasting legacy, every year the best collegiate linebacker in the country receives the Butkus Award.

Position: **Linebacker**
Hometown: **Chicago, IL**
Born: **Dec. 9, 1942**
Died: **Oct. 5, 2023**
Height: **6'3"**
Weight: **245 lbs.**
Team: **Chicago Bears (1965–73)**
Career Fumble Recoveries: **25**

Darrell Green

Darrell Green wasn't blessed with size. As a middle schooler in Houston in the early 1970s, Darrell actually played football for the local elementary school. "Instead of playing with guys my age, I played with the guys my size," the 5'9" Hall of Fame cornerback said.

By the time he reached eighth grade, however, Darrell was too old to play with the elementary school kids. Being a bit intimidated at the prospect of going up against kids much bigger than himself, Darrell took a little hiatus from football to focus on a sport where size was less important: track.

As it turned out, Darrell was blessed with speed, and plenty of it. At Jesse H. Jones High School, he blossomed as a sprinter, earning All-State honors. Still, in his heart, he was a football player, and having used track to establish his athletic bona fides, he decided to give football another go during his junior year. He was put on the junior varsity team.

The next year, Darrell finally got his chance to shine on the varsity level. He played well enough to be named to the All-City team, but he didn't garner much attention from any major college. Division II Texas A&I (now known as Texas A&M-Kingsville) offered him the opportunity to run track and play football, and Green took it.

In college, Green's elite athleticism was on full display. During his senior year, he was a Division II All-American cornerback and the Lone Star Conference Defensive Player of the Year. His star shone even brighter on the track, where he clocked a 10.08-second 100-meter-dash time. The only collegiate athlete with a faster time was future Olympic gold medalist Carl Lewis.

As he entered the 1983 NFL draft, questions about Green's size persisted. Fresh off a Super Bowl victory, the Washington Redskins could afford to take some risks, and they selected Green with the 28th pick. He quickly established himself as the NFL's fastest man. The very first time he touched the ball as a pro–in a preseason game against the Atlanta Falcons–he fielded a punt and returned it 61 yards for a touchdown. Later that year, he made jaws drop by coming all the way across the field to run down Tony Dorsett, the Dallas Cowboys' speedy running back.

Suffice it to say, Green turned out to be worth the gamble. Despite his diminutive stature, he had a whale of a career. Consistent and durable, Green remained a fixture in Washington's secondary for 20 years, winning two Super Bowls along the way. He was a starter until age 40 and set an NFL record of at least one interception in 19 consecutive seasons.

He retired in 2002 at the age of 42. He was a seven-time Pro Bowler and was named a first-team All-Pro once. He finished his career with 54 interceptions, not including the six he recorded in the playoffs. Darrell Green–the man people said was too small to play football–was inducted into the Hall of Fame in 2008.

Position: **Cornerback**
Hometown: **Houston, TX**
Born: **Feb. 15, 1960**
Height: **5'9"**
Weight: **184 lbs.**
Team: **Washington Redskins (1983–2002)**
Career Interceptions: **54**

Rob Gronkowski

Long before tight end Rob Gronkowski (nick-named "Gronk") had to survive the bone-crunching blows of NFL defenders, he had to face down an even more menacing crew: his four brothers. And if even half of the stories from his childhood are true, it's a wonder the five-time Pro Bowler survived to adulthood.

Gordy Gronkowski and Diane Gronkowski Walters knew how to produce athletes. Their five sons, who range from 6'2" to 6'6", all played professionally in one form or another. Having that many large, athletic, competitive boys in a con-fined space resulted in nothing less than chaos.

Brawls between brothers broke out on a near-daily basis, and Rob, who was the second young-est, always seemed to be in the middle of them. To be fair, Gordy didn't do much to discourage his boys' aggressiveness. To settle disputes, he'd clear out the furniture in the living room, set his combatant sons in separate corners, give them each a couch pillow, and let them charge at one another until they settled matters. There were only two rules: no shots to the head and no hits below the belt.

Even in a family of hulks, Rob was different. Fearless, he seemed to relish pain. He would insti-gate; get beaten down by his three older brothers; and then, with a smile and a laugh, instigate some more. His relentless energy may have driven his parents crazy, but it served him well on the foot-ball field.

Rob grew until he was 6'6" and weighed 268 pounds. He was fast, could catch anything, and was extremely flexible. He starred for Williamsville North High School in New York before finishing

high school at Woodland Hills in Pennsylvania. Heavily recruited, Gronkowski chose to play college at the University of Arizona. He made his presence felt immediately, catching 28 balls for 525 yards and six touchdowns as a freshman.

He caught 10 more touchdowns his sophomore season but missed his entire junior year because of a back injury. That didn't stop Gronkowski from declaring for the 2010 NFL draft, but the injury did likely prevent him from becoming a first-round pick. The New England Patriots ended up select-ing him with the 42nd overall pick.

Gronkowski gelled well with Patriots all-world quarterback Tom Brady, and he proved to be a touchdown machine. After finding pay dirt 10 times as a rookie, Gronk established himself as the league's premier tight end during his second professional season. That year, he set a record for tight ends by catching 17 touchdown passes. In the process, he became the first tight end to lead the league in touchdown receptions.

Gronk caught 38 touchdowns in just his first three years with the Patriots. No other tight end had more than 25 in that same period. He won three Super Bowls with the Patriots before retiring following the 2018 season. After sitting out a year, Gronk joined Brady's new team, the Tampa Bay Buccaneers. There, Gronk won his fourth Lombardi Trophy.

Gronk retired for good after the 2021 season, having been named a first-team All-Pro four times. His 93 career touchdowns rank third all-time for his position, and he is a near-lock to make the Hall of Fame when he becomes eligible in 2027.

Position: **Tight End**
Hometown: **Amherst, NY**
Born: **May 14, 1989**
Height: **6'6"**
Weight: **265 lbs.**
Teams: **New England Patriots (2010–18), Tampa Bay Buccaneers (2020–21)**
Career Receiving Yards: **9,286**

Devin Hester

In the lead-up to Super Bowl XLI, the Indianapolis Colts had a decision to make. Their opponent, the Chicago Bears, possessed one of the most electrifying—and dangerous—weapons in the NFL: rookie return specialist Devin Hester.

During the regular season, the former University of Miami Hurricane had taken the league by storm, setting the single-season record for most nonoffensive touchdowns. Hester, who could reach his top speed at a superhuman rate, had returned three punts, two kickoffs, and one missed field goal attempt for scores. His heroics helped catapult Chicago to its first Super Bowl appearance in 21 years. But would Indianapolis even give Hester a chance to perform on the sport's biggest stage? Or would they decide to kick the ball anywhere but in Hester's direction?

The Colts chose poorly. They sent the opening kickoff to Hester, who promptly returned it 92 yards for a touchdown. The 14-second sequence marked the fastest touchdown in Super Bowl history. And in just one season, Hester officially cemented himself as an NFL legend.

One year previously, it was Hester who had a decision to make: return to Miami for his senior year or declare for the NFL draft. On one hand, he had promised his father Lenorris Hester Sr. that he would earn his college degree. This was no ordinary promise either. Lenorris had died of cancer at 33 when Devin was 12 years old, and his dying wish was for his son to get an education.

On the other hand, Hurricane Frances had ravaged Hester's home in 2004, and an NFL con-

tract could go a long way in helping his mother Juanita Brown rebuild. Hester had already watched his mom overcome so much. In 1993, a car accident had almost paralyzed her, leaving her bedridden for weeks. Devin, along with his older brother Lenorris Jr. and younger sister Keaundra, had to help her with everything—even with going to the bathroom. It took her years to make a full recovery.

All that adversity taught young Devin to keep fighting and to dream big. So after searching his heart, Hester decided helping his family was most important, and he declared for the 2006 NFL draft. The Bears selected him in the second round.

He quickly proved he belonged in the league, returning a punt 84 yards for a touchdown against the Bears' hated rival, the Green Bay Packers, in his pro debut. His record-setting rookie year led to a Pro Bowl berth and a first-team All-Pro designation. And Hester was just getting started. He returned six more kicks for touchdowns in 2007 and in 2011 broke the NFL all-time record for punt return TDs.

Hester retired in 2016 with a myriad of NFL records, including most nonoffensive touchdowns in a career (20), most kickoff and punt return touchdowns (19), and most punt return touchdowns (14). It is rare for a special teams player to make such a profound impact on the field. Then again, Devin Hester was a rare talent indeed.

Position: **Returner**

Hometown: **Riviera Beach, FL**

Born: **Nov. 4, 1982**

Height: **5'11"**

Weight: **190 lbs.**

Teams: **Chicago Bears (2006–13), Atlanta Falcons (2014–15), Baltimore Ravens (2016), Seattle Seahawks (2016)**

Career Return Touchdowns: **20**

Deacon Jones

Riffling through the Los Angeles phone book, David Jones noted he shared a name with a lot of people –too many for his liking. The Los Angeles Rams defensive end wanted to stand out and decided to give himself a nickname. He settled on "Deacon," reasoning that such a name would be remembered. He was correct.

Deacon Jones's path to NFL greatness was long, winding, and riddled with the same type of potholes that every Black person encountered in the segregated South of the first half of the 20th century. He was born on December 9, 1938, in Eatonville, Florida, to a family with little means. His parents ran a barbecue stand, and he picked watermelons in the summer to help support his family.

Though he played football at Hungerford High School, he didn't receive any scholarships, so he hitched a ride to New York to find work. However, a job never materialized, and practically starving, he made his way back to Florida.

Out of the blue, South Carolina State University offered him a football scholarship. While there, Jones participated in a lunch counter march after some Black students were denied service. When the school found out about his participation in the demonstration, it revoked his scholarship.

His next offer came from Mississippi Vocational after an SCSU assistant took a job there. But when the school uncovered Jones's history of civil disobedience, it sent a police squad to escort him and some of his teammates to the state border. The police warned them not to come to Mississippi again. For the rest of his life, Jones never did.

That could have been it for him. However, some Los Angeles Rams scouts were watching film of a couple of running back prospects when they noticed a 6'4", 272-pound defensive tackle outrunning the backs. They recommended taking a chance on the defender, and in the 14th round of the 1961 NFL draft, the Rams selected Deacon Jones.

Jones's emotions about all the injustice he had witnessed motivated him. "If I did not have football then, I'd probably have been in jail because I did have a lot of anger in me," he said. Luckily, he had an outlet on the gridiron. It was soon apparent that this unheralded, inexperienced player had greatness in him also.

Jones made it his mission to pressure NFL quarterbacks. To get to them, he would slap offensive linemen on the side of their helmets to stun them and gain the advantage. His head slaps were so devastating that the league eventually outlawed them. Back then, there wasn't a term for tackling the quarterback behind the line of scrimmage. It was Jones himself who coined the word *sack*. Though the sack didn't become an official statistic until 1982, it is believed he would have had 194.5 of them in his career.

In Los Angeles, Jones was part of a dominating defensive line known as the "Fearsome Foursome." During this time, Jones made seven consecutive Pro Bowls from 1964 to 1970 and was a first-team All-Pro five straight seasons from 1965 to 1969. He retired in 1974 and was inducted into the Hall of Fame in 1980.

He passed away on June 3, 2013, from natural causes at the age of 74 years.

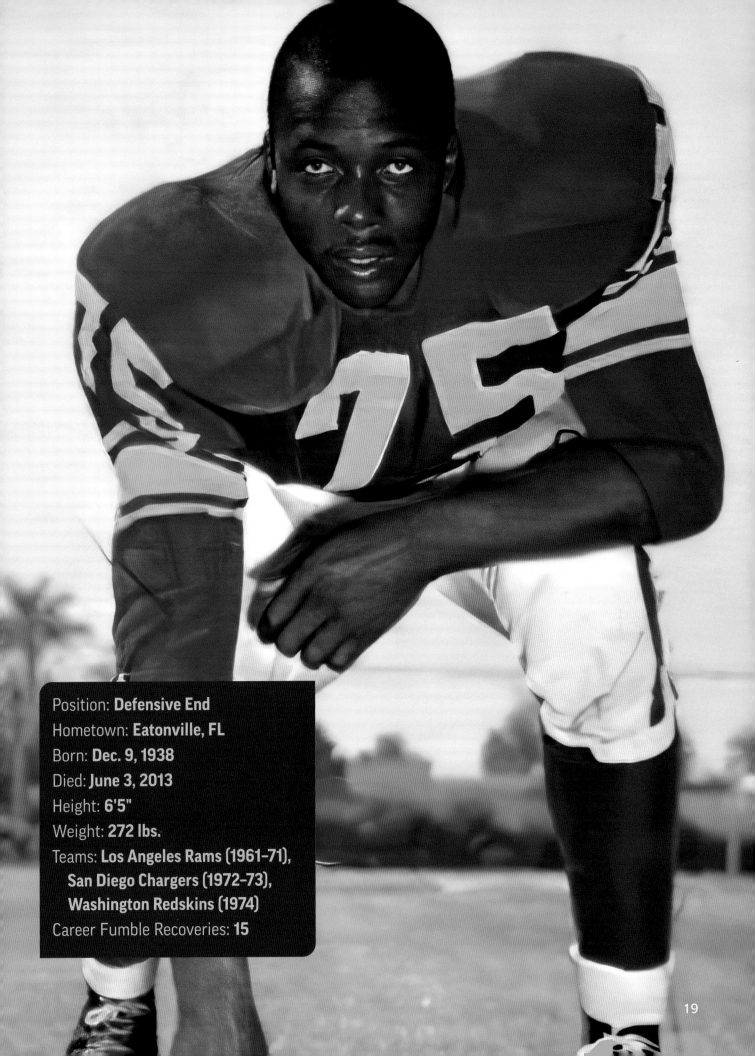

Position: **Defensive End**
Hometown: **Eatonville, FL**
Born: **Dec. 9, 1938**
Died: **June 3, 2013**
Height: **6'5"**
Weight: **272 lbs.**
Teams: **Los Angeles Rams (1961–71),**
San Diego Chargers (1972–73),
Washington Redskins (1974)
Career Fumble Recoveries: **15**

Jack Lambert

Following his freshman year at Crestwood High School in Mantua, Ohio, Jack Lambert asked his coach if he could change his number to 00. "If you want to wear a special number, you've got to be a special player," the coach told him. Jack got the number after his sophomore season. Just how special was he? The school has since retired that number, and its football team now plays at Jack Lambert Stadium.

Even though Jack earned nine letters at Crestwood for his efforts on the football, basketball, and baseball teams, the future Pittsburgh Steelers Hall of Fame middle linebacker struggled to get noticed beyond Mantua, a small town with a population back then of about 1,200 in the northeast part of the state.

Born July 8, 1952, to Jack Lambert Sr. and Joyce Brehm, the boy worked on his grandfather's farm during his childhood summers. The experience of driving a tractor, baling hay, and performing other odd jobs gave Jack, as his mother put it, "farm-boy strength." He used that strength to deliver bone-crushing hits on the football field. A cornerback for Crestwood, Jack hit so hard that opposing teams stopped throwing the ball in his direction.

Colleges, however, were not so impressed. They considered Lambert too slow to play cornerback at the next level, and at 170 pounds, they considered him too small to play any other position. Eventually, Kent State University gave him an opportunity. Before Lambert's junior year in 1972, KSU's new coach Don James decided to move him from defensive end to linebacker. Lambert's play made James look like a genius.

That season, Lambert led the Mid-American Conference with 233 tackles on his way to being named the conference's Defensive Player of the Year. His senior year, he helped lead the Golden Flashes to their best record in school history at 9–2. For the second straight year, he was a first-team All-MAC selection. The Steelers drafted Lambert in the second round of the 1974 NFL draft.

Pittsburgh's incumbent middle linebacker Henry Davis was a Pro Bowl–level player, and Lambert seemed destined to begin his career as a backup. However, in the preseason, Davis suffered a nerve injury in his neck, and Lambert was inserted into the starting lineup. Immediately, he became a key cog in Pittsburgh's vaunted "Steel Curtain" defense, which led the Steelers to Super Bowl victories in Lambert's first two seasons.

As the Steelers established themselves as the NFL's premier franchise, Lambert established himself as the game's premier linebacker. After winning Defensive Rookie of the Year in 1974, he made nine straight Pro Bowls beginning in 1975. He was the Defensive Player of the Year in 1976 and a six-time first-team All-Pro selection. The Steelers would win four Super Bowls in Lambert's career, which ended following the 1984 season.

Lambert's tough, physical play made him an intimidating presence on the field that was only magnified by his appearance. A collision on the basketball court in high school had knocked out his front four teeth, giving him an almost vampire-like look whenever he bared his teeth. It was an image that no doubt gave opponents nightmares. Lambert was inducted into the Hall of Fame in 1990.

Position: **Linebacker**
Hometown: **Mantua, OH**
Born: **July 8, 1952**
Height: **6'4"**
Weight: **220 lbs.**
Team: **Pittsburgh Steelers
 (1974–84)**
Career Interceptions: **28**

Steve Largent

As a kid growing up in Oklahoma City, Steve Largent didn't just love football—he needed it. At the time, he was dealing with an extremely turbulent homelife. Steve's parents divorced when he was six, and the man his mom later married was an alcoholic who could become argumentative and abusive. On many occasions, Steve would cry himself to sleep.

To escape the stress of his stepfather, the future Hall of Fame wide receiver threw himself into athletics. As a student at Putnam City High School, Steve would go out and catch 300 balls each day during the offseason, putting in the time and effort one would expect from a professional player.

While Steve definitely wanted to earn a college scholarship, his drive stemmed from something even more basic. Desperate for a loving father figure in his life, Steve did everything he could to win the respect and affections of his coaches. He successfully developed a close relationship with Putnam football coach Jerry Potter and, as a result, Steve worked as hard as he could for Potter.

Though he had a standout high school career, neither Oklahoma University nor Oklahoma State University recruited him. He did, however, catch the eye of the coaches at the University of Tulsa, and when he graduated in 1972, Largent continued his football career as a Golden Hurricane.

At Tulsa, Largent put up some big numbers. He led the nation in receiving touchdowns his junior year with 14, and he repeated the feat as a senior in 1975. Even so, at 5'11" and 187 pounds, most scouts considered him too small—and slow—for the NFL. Largent had to wait until the fourth round of the 1976 draft before the Houston Oilers selected him.

Largent's stint in Houston was brief. After the Oilers' final preseason game, the franchise decided their rookie receiver didn't fit into the team's plans. They intended to release him when the NFL's newest franchise, the Seattle Seahawks, showed interest. About to start its inaugural season, Seattle was looking for talent anywhere it could find it, and one of its coaches happened to be a former Tulsa assistant. At his urging, Seattle traded an eighth round draft pick to Houston for Largent.

Seattle wouldn't regret it. Largent quickly established himself as the team's best receiver. What he lacked in terms of size and raw athleticism, he made up for with his precise route running and stickum hands. In his third year, he became Seattle's first-ever Pro Bowler, an honor he would achieve six more times in his 14-year career.

A model of consistency, Largent surpassed 1,000 receiving yards every year from 1978 through 1986 except for the strike-shortened 1982 season. He twice led the league in receiving yards—in 1979 and 1985. In 1989, his final season, he caught his 100th touchdown pass, surpassing Don Hutson's 44-year NFL record.

At his retirement, he owned six major career receiving records: most receptions (819), most consecutive games with a reception (177), most receiving yards (13,089), most receiving touchdowns (100), most seasons with at least 50 receptions (10), and most 1,000-yard seasons (8). Largent was inducted into the NFL Hall of Fame in 1995.

Position: **Wide Receiver**
Hometown: **Tulsa, OK**
Born: **Sept. 28, 1954**
Height: **5'11"**
Weight: **187 lbs.**
Team: **Seattle Seahawks (1976–89)**
Career Receptions: **819**

Ray Lewis

Sunseria Jenkins asked a lot from the eldest of her five children. Jenkins was just 16 when Ray Lewis was born on May 15, 1975, in Bartow, Florida. The boy's father wasn't around. In fact, Ray didn't meet Elbert Ray Jackson until he was in high school. For much of his childhood, Ray was the man of the house, and his mother relied on him.

It fell on the future Baltimore Ravens linebacker to help his sisters with their hair and make sure his younger brother got to day care on time. Ray learned how to cook noodles and oatmeal for his siblings. He cleaned the house. For her part, Jenkins was a strict disciplinarian determined to make sure her kids avoided the trouble that befell so many in their neighborhood. Life could be a struggle, and watching his mom fight through it instilled in Ray a strong desire to make things easier for her.

At times, Jenkins felt she took Ray's childhood away from him because of all she put on his shoulders. But there was one thing that allowed Ray to feel carefree and just be a kid: pickup football games in the parks and streets of his neighborhood. It was during one of those games Ray's athleticism caught the eye of a local youth coach, who persuaded Jenkins to allow her 10-year-old son to sign up for organized football.

By the time Ray got to Kathleen High School, his talent was apparent. As a sophomore, he impressed coaches with his ability to pick things up quickly, his natural aggressiveness, and his love of practice. The linebacker made plays all over the field, drawing the attention of several big-name colleges. Ray's decision came down to Florida State University and the University of Miami. Ray chose the Hurricanes after an FSU coach offended him during a recruiting visit by telling him he wouldn't be able to start his first two years.

At Miami, Lewis proved he didn't need two years of seasoning by earning freshman All-American honors. The next two years, he was named a first-team All-American, and he declared for the NFL draft following his junior season. The Baltimore Ravens selected Lewis with the 26th overall pick of the 1996 draft, and he would be a mainstay of their defense for the next 17 years.

Lewis made three Pro Bowls in his first four years, but his true breakout season came in 2000. The middle linebacker led what is considered one of the best defenses in NFL history. The 2000 Ravens set records for fewest rushing yards and fewest points allowed during a 16-game season. Lewis recorded 137 total tackles, three sacks, and two interceptions on his way to being NFL Defensive Player of the Year. He also earned Super Bowl MVP honors after the Ravens dismantled the New York Giants 34–7 to win the franchise's first title.

His dominance continued for a dozen more years, and in his final season, the 2012 Ravens once again became Super Bowl champions, holding off the San Francisco 49ers 34–31 and allowing Lewis to retire on top. Lewis made 12 Pro Bowls and was a first-team All-Pro seven times. He was inducted into the Hall of Fame in 2018.

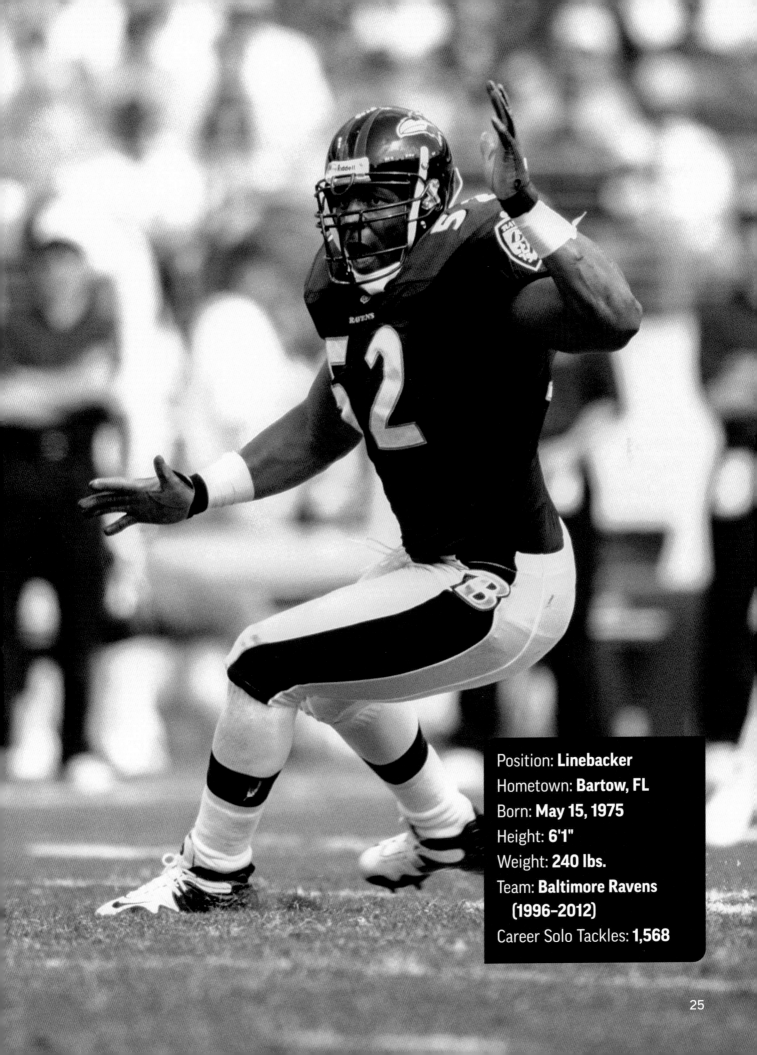

Position: **Linebacker**
Hometown: **Bartow, FL**
Born: **May 15, 1975**
Height: **6'1"**
Weight: **240 lbs.**
Team: **Baltimore Ravens
(1996–2012)**
Career Solo Tackles: **1,568**

Ronnie Lott

The story is as legendary as the player. During the last week of the 1985 season, San Francisco 49ers safety Ronnie Lott dislocated and tore the tip of his left pinky finger while tackling Dallas Cowboys running back Timmy Newsome. Doctors recommended reconstructive surgery, which would have required a long recovery period and caused Lott to miss some of the 1986 season.

Instead of surgery, Lott opted to have part of his injured finger amputated. Because of this drastic decision, Lott was ready for the start of training camp. And after that he produced what may have been the finest season of his Hall of Fame career. In 1986, Lott led the league with 10 interceptions while forcing three fumbles and scoring a touchdown on his way to being named a first-team All-Pro.

Though he later expressed some regret about taking such an extreme measure just to stay on the field, the decision to amputate over surgery was on brand for Lott, who was known for his ferocity. Famous for his punishing hits, Lott once compared being tackled by him to being struck hard with a baseball bat. Hall of Fame coach Tom Landry said Lott was "like a middle linebacker playing safety."

Ronald Mandel Lott was born on May 8, 1959, in Albuquerque, New Mexico. His father Roy was an officer in the Air Force while his mother Mary was a stay-at-home mom. The nature of Roy's job meant Ronnie moved several times as a kid. When Ronnie was four, the Lotts moved to the Washington, DC, area. At nine, Ronnie and his two siblings were uprooted to Rialto, California.

It was there that Ronnie would begin to make a name for himself. At Eisenhower High School, he lettered in basketball, baseball, and football, but his most significant honor came when he was named a *Parade* magazine High School All-American in football.

Upon graduating high school in 1977, Lott decided to continue playing football at the University of Southern California. The Trojans won the national championship in 1978 and nearly repeated the next year. In 1980, Lott was a unanimous All-American selection. As if that weren't impressive enough, he even played in six games for the school's basketball team during the 1979–80 season.

San Francisco took Lott as the eighth pick of the 1981 NFL draft, and he made an immediate impact. The 49ers switched Lott to cornerback, and the rookie started every game, playing well enough to make the Pro Bowl while also being named a first-team All-Pro. To top it off, San Francisco won the franchise's first Super Bowl.

Lott moved to free safety in 1985, and from 1986 to 1991, he made the Pro Bowl each season and was a first-team All-Pro five times. In his 10 seasons with the 49ers, Lott won four Super Bowls. Prior to the 1991 season, he signed with the Raiders, who moved him to strong safety. Lott once again led the NFL in interceptions and was named a first-team All-Pro at his third position. He finished his career with the New York Jets in 1994.

In 14 NFL seasons, Lott made 10 Pro Bowls and six first-team All-Pro teams. He was inducted into the Hall of Fame in 2000.

Position: **Safety/Cornerback**

Hometown: **Albuquerque, NM**

Born: **May 8, 1959**

Height: **6'**

Weight: **203 lbs.**

Teams: **San Francisco 49ers (1981–90),**
   Los Angeles Raiders (1991–92),
   New York Jets (1993–94)

Career Interceptions: **63**

Peyton Manning

Indianapolis Colts quarterback coach Bruce Arians made a habit of never leaving the team facility before all the players had gone home. He thought it set an example about dedication to his profession. Then, with the first pick of the 1998 NFL draft, the Colts selected quarterback Peyton Manning out of the University of Tennessee, and Arians's philosophy was soon put to the test.

At the time, the coach's other ritual was to take his wife out to dinner on Thursdays, the only night he had available amid his busy schedule. But his new quarterback had some habits of his own, one of which was to stay at the team facility late into the night watching game film and thinking up novel ways to defeat NFL defenses. For Arians, something had to give: his rule of being the last one out of the building or his date night with his wife.

Wisely, Arians chose his wife over his young quarterback. The coach was perhaps the first to learn what the entire league was about to find out. While preparation is important to everybody in the NFL, nobody prepared quite like Peyton Manning.

Manning's obsessive and meticulous habits didn't start when he reached the NFL. The son of former NFL quarterback Archie Manning, Peyton loved nothing more than watching game film with his father as a child growing up in New Orleans. As a teenager, Peyton looked at film daily. "Son, get a girlfriend," the elder Manning would say. "You need to get out more." His son's reply? "Daddy, I've got to watch film."

Undoubtedly, Peyton had some inherent advantages over the average kid with professional aspirations by having an NFL quarterback for a father. However, he was not particularly fast or strong. But he relentlessly strove for perfection. At Isidore Newman School, a private school Peyton attended from kindergarten to high school, he would organize impromptu workouts with his receivers, having them run routes over and over and over again.

The hard work paid off. In 1993, Peyton was the Gatorade Circle of Champions National High School Player of the Year. He made the surprise decision to attend Tennessee, spurning his father's alma mater Ole Miss. As a Volunteer, he finished his four-year career with a 39–6 record, throwing for a Southeastern Conference record 11,201 yards, along with 89 touchdowns.

His success continued in the NFL. After going 3–13 his rookie year, Manning led the Colts to a 13–3 record in 1999. With Manning at the helm, the Colts would record double-digit victories every year from 1999 through 2010, except in 2001. In his 17 seasons, he was a five-time MVP, 14-time Pro Bowler, seven-time first-team All-Pro and two-time Super Bowl champion.

When he retired following the 2015 season, Manning held the NFL record for career passing yards (71,940), career passing touchdowns (539), single-season passing touchdowns (55), and single-season passing yards (5,477). In the process, he helped transform the NFL from a run-first league into one dominated by quarterbacks. From 1990 to 2000, five running backs won the MVP Award. Over the next 20 seasons, 17 quarterbacks accepted the honor. Manning was inducted into the Hall of Fame in 2021.

Position: **Quarterback**

Hometown: **New Orleans, LA**

Born: **Mar. 24, 1976**

Height: **6'5"**

Weight: **230 lbs.**

Teams: **Indianapolis Colts (1998–2010), Denver Broncos (2012–15)**

Career Passing Touchdowns: **539**

Bruce Matthews

Six of former NFL player William Clay Matthews Sr.'s direct descendants went on to have successful NFL careers. Among them, though, William's youngest son Bruce stands above the rest. In his 19 seasons as an offensive lineman for the Houston Oilers/Tennessee Titans, the Hall of Famer appeared in 296 games–about 30 games more than any other lineman in history.

Bruce Matthews played so long that his final head coach, Jeff Fisher, was one of his former college teammates at the University of Southern California. And he was productive to the very end. In Matthews's final season, which came in 2001 when he was 40 years old, the ageless warrior was named to his 14th consecutive Pro Bowl. That number is exceeded only by Tom Brady's 15 Pro Bowls.

Bruce wasn't the first of William's four sons to play professional football. His older brother Clay was a first-round pick of the Cleveland Browns five years before Houston made Bruce the ninth overall player selected in the 1983 draft. Clay, a linebacker who made four Pro Bowls himself, also played 19 seasons.

The competition between Bruce and his older brother preceded–and extended far beyond–football. Basketball games between them generally turned into shouting matches, with the occasional black eye, busted lip, or bloody nose thrown in for good measure.

Their competitive nature came from William, who lettered in football, wrestling, and swimming at Georgia Tech before playing for the San Francisco 49ers in the early 1950s. As a senior in college, William won Georgia's Golden Gloves heavyweight boxing championship the night before winning the Southeastern Conference's heavyweight wrestling title.

After his NFL career, William moved his family to several locations around the country as he climbed various corporate ladders. Bruce started high school in Illinois before finishing as an All-American at Arcadia High School in California. Like his brother before him, Bruce then went on to be an All-American at USC.

Houston was a bottom-feeder during Matthews's first few years, but in 1987 the team began a run of seven-straight years of making the playoffs. The team's success coincided with Matthews's individual success. His first Pro Bowl came six years into his career, in 1988. But from that point forward he was a Pro Bowler for the rest of his career. In that span, he was also named a first-team All-Pro seven times. He was inducted into the Hall of Fame in 2007.

NFL success for the Matthews family didn't stop with Bruce and Clay's generation. Two of Clay's sons–Clay Matthews III and Casey Matthews–played linebacker in the NFL. Bruce has also put two sons in the league: Jake is a starter on the Atlanta Falcons' offensive line while Kevin played a couple of seasons at center for Tennessee.

Position: **Offensive Lineman**

Hometown: **Raleigh, NC**

Born: **August 8, 1961**

Height: **6'5"**

Weight: **305 lbs.**

Team: **Houston Oilers/Tennessee Titans (1983–2001)**

Fact: **Played in 296 games**

Joe Montana

San Francisco 49ers quarterback Joe Montana was on the verge of losing a Super Bowl for the first time in his career. With 3:04 seconds left in Super Bowl XXIII, the 49ers trailed the Cincinnati Bengals by three and were backed up on their own eight-yard line.

With all the pressure in the world upon him, Montana confidently strode to the huddle and pointed out to his anxious teammates that movie star John Candy was sitting in the stands on the far side of the field. Montana then calmly led his team on an 11-play, 92-yard drive, connecting on eight of nine passes, with his final one finding John Taylor in the end zone for the game-winning touchdown.

They didn't call him Joe Cool for nothing.

Joe Montana Jr. was born on June 11, 1956, in New Eagle, Pennsylvania, which lies in the southwestern part of the state. Western Pennsylvania has been called the "Cradle of Quarterbacks," as legends such as Johnny Unitas, Joe Namath, Jim Kelly, and Dan Marino all hail from that region. Montana's legacy would outshine them all.

The only child of Joseph Sr. and Theresa Montana, Joe was particularly close to his father. Joe Sr. said he never had anyone to throw a ball around with growing up, and he didn't want that for his son. The younger Joe would wait at the door, ball in hand, for his dad to come home from work. His father signed Joe up for sports early–literally. Joe began playing peewee football at eight, even though the legal age limit was nine, after his father fudged Joe's age on the sign-up form.

Joe excelled at all sports. In Little League baseball, he pitched three perfect games. He played basketball well enough that North Carolina State offered him a scholarship. But Joe was from Western Pennsylvania, and that meant quarterbacking was in his blood. He idolized a local boy named Terry Hanratty, who went on to play quarterback at Notre Dame. So when the Fighting Irish offered Joe the chance to do the same, he jumped at the opportunity.

Montana led the Irish to a National Championship in 1977, but because NFL scouts labeled him as having "average" arm strength, Montana wasn't drafted until the third round in 1979. In 14 seasons with the 49ers, Montana led them to four Super Bowl titles. For his career, he was an eight-time Pro Bowler, three-time All-Pro, and two-time MVP.

And Joe Cool always saved his best for the biggest stage. In his four Super Bowl appearances, Montana completed 68 percent of his passes for 1,142 yards, 11 touchdowns–and zero interceptions. Most importantly, he walked away the champion all four times.

Montana was elected to the Hall of Fame in 2000.

Position: **Quarterback**
Hometown: **New Eagle, PA**
Born: **June 11, 1956**
Height: **6'2"**
Weight: **200 lbs.**
Teams: **San Francisco 49ers (1979–90, 1992), Kansas City Chiefs (1993–94)**
Super Bowl QB Rating: **127.8**

Randy Moss

Randy Moss felt he should be a Dallas Cowboy. Leading up to the 1998 NFL draft, the All-American wide receiver from Marshall University thought he had received assurances from the franchise that it would select him with the eighth pick.

However, when the time came, the Cowboys chose defensive end Greg Ellis. After that, team after team passed on the player who rewrote the Thundering Herd record book and finished fourth in Heisman Trophy voting in 1997. The Minnesota Vikings finally put a stop to Moss's free fall, choosing him with the 21st pick.

Moss vowed to make all the teams that had passed on him regret it. But there was no team he wanted to embarrass more than Dallas.

On paper, it seemed preposterous that a player of his caliber would last until pick 21. In 28 games at Marshall, Moss had scored 54 touchdowns, recording at least one touchdown in every collegiate game in which he played.

The Rand, West Virginia, native possessed an unstoppable combination of size—at 6'4"—and speed—a blistering sub-4.3-second 40-yard dash. Anyone big enough to guard him couldn't keep up; anyone fast enough was too small to challenge him for the ball.

At DuPont High School, Randy was twice named West Virginia Basketball Player of the Year, but it was his production on the football field that garnered national attention. The Panthers won back-to-back state titles with Randy leading the way, and then–Notre Dame coach Lou Holtz called Randy the best player he had ever seen on film. The young player was determined to join the Fighting Irish, going so far as hiring a tutor to help prepare him for the SATs.

Moss would never make it to South Bend, though. The event that led the generational talent to unheralded Marshall is the same one that later scared so many NFL teams away. During his senior year at DuPont, Randy was part of a fight that landed a kid in the hospital. The kid allegedly wrote derogatory words about Black people on the desk of Randy's girlfriend. Though nobody could deny his talents, both collegiate and pro teams considered him too risky of an investment.

Minnesota took the plunge at the NFL draft–and was rewarded for it. In his first game, Moss caught four passes for 95 yards and two touchdowns. By the time of the Vikings' Thanksgiving Day clash against the Cowboys, Moss was already a sensation. But his exploits that day made him a legend. His stat line in the victory: three catches for 163 yards and three touchdowns.

Over his 14-year career that spanned five franchises, Moss made six Pro Bowls and four first-team All-Pro selections. His 156 receiving touchdowns trail only Jerry Rice, while his 15,292 receiving yards are fourth all-time. He was enshrined in the Hall of Fame in 2018.

And he never lost to the Dallas Cowboys.

Position: **Wide Receiver**

Hometown: **Rand, WV**

Born: **Feb. 13, 1977**

Height: **6'4"**

Weight: **210 lbs.**

Teams: **Minnesota Vikings (1998–2004, 2010), Oakland Raiders (2005–6), New England Patriots (2007–9, 2010), Tennessee Titans (2010), San Francisco 49ers (2012)**

Career Receiving Yards: **15,292**

Anthony Muñoz

In the first game of Anthony Muñoz's senior year at the University of Southern California, the All-American left tackle sustained a knee injury that required major reconstructive surgery. His coaches encouraged him to petition the Pac-10 Conference for another year of eligibility, assuming his season was over. Muñoz would hear nothing of it.

He announced he would play again that season—a proclamation nobody believed possible or took seriously. And yet, in the 1980 Rose Bowl, which pitted the Trojans against the Buckeyes of Ohio State a mere fourth months after the injury, there was Muñoz, throwing the crucial block that cleared running back Charles White for the game-winning touchdown. Nobody tells Muñoz he can't do something.

That knee injury wasn't the first of Muñoz's college career, nor was it the second. It was the third. So even though the 6'6", 278-pound unstoppable force had been dominant when healthy enough to play, NFL teams didn't consider him a sure thing because of his history of injuries. It just so happened, though, that Cincinnati Bengals founder Paul Brown and his two sons were at that Rose Bowl game, and they were blown away by Muñoz. With the third pick of the 1980 NFL draft, the Bengals took a swing with Muñoz—and hit a home run.

Actually, Anthony Muñoz's first love had been baseball. Born on August 19, 1958, in Ontario, California, Anthony and his four siblings were raised by their mom Esther after their father split. While Esther worked at a local farm packing eggs into cartons, Anthony spent a good portion of his childhood riding his bike from one baseball game to the next. By the age of five, he already was the size of a typical nine-year-old, and everybody wanted Anthony on their team.

The boy kept growing until he became too big *not* to play football. But he never lost his passion for baseball. He only agreed to play football for USC after the coaches promised to let him suit up with the school's baseball team in the spring. Though the rehabilitation of his various knee injuries kept him from playing baseball most of his time in college, he did pitch for the Trojans' 1978 national championship team.

As fragile as Muñoz's knees were in college, they were just the opposite in the NFL. He kept himself in top-notch shape by lifting weights several times per week and running three to four miles each day. As a result, he missed just three games due to injury in his entire 13-year career. In the process, he established himself as one of the best offensive linemen the game had ever seen.

Agile, quick, and strong, Muñoz proved to be an exceptional blocker. He was so athletic, he even caught seven passes while scoring four touchdowns on tackle-eligible plays throughout his career. He made the Pro Bowl each year from 1981 to 1991 and was a first-team All-Pro selection nine times over that stretch. He was the NFL Offensive Lineman of the Year three times and named the Walter Payton NFL Man of the Year in 1991.

Muñoz was inducted into the Hall of Fame in 1998, becoming the first player of primarily Hispanic descent to enter the Hall.

Position: **Offensive Tackle**

Hometown: **Ontario, CA**

Born: **Aug. 19, 1958**

Height: **6'6"**

Weight: **278 lbs.**

Team: **Cincinnati Bengals (1980–92)**

Fact: **Caught 4 touchdowns as an OT**

Alan Page

Alan Page's list of accomplishments is quite impressive. During his 11-plus seasons with the Minnesota Vikings, the defensive tackle made nine Pro Bowls and was named a first-team All-Pro five times. In 1971, he became the first defensive player to win the NFL's MVP Award. Page helped lead the Vikings to 10 division titles and four Super Bowl appearances. In 1988, he was inducted into the Pro Football Hall of Fame, which happens to be in Page's hometown of Canton, Ohio.

For most players, all of that would represent life-defining achievements. For Page, however, they are merely footnotes. The impact he has made off the field far exceeds anything he accomplished on it. That's because in 1992, Hall of Fame football star Alan Page was elected to the Supreme Court of Minnesota, and, in the process, became the first Black person to hold a major state office in Minnesota.

Alan Page's interest in law started early. Born on August 7, 1945, Alan was eight years old when the U.S. Supreme Court decided in *Brown v. Board of Education* that racially segregated schools were unconstitutional. From that, Alan first sensed that the law was powerful and could be used to make the country a fairer place. That the case centered on educational opportunities for minorities was quite appropriate because nothing in the Page household was as sacred as education.

Alan's father Howard was a bartender who hadn't gone beyond high school, and his mother Georgianna worked as a country club attendant. They hammered home a simple message to their four children: Education is the key to a better life.

Practicing what they preached, they sent their children to Central Catholic High School despite the tuition costs because Georgianna considered it better than the local public schools.

Alan excelled on Central Catholic's football team, but even back then he was uncomfortable with what he called "the phenomenon of athlete worship," reasoning that one's performance on the field doesn't speak to a person's character off it. He went on to play at the University of Notre Dame, helping lead the Irish to undefeated national titles in 1964 and 1966. Minnesota drafted him with the 15th pick of the 1967 draft.

He became a starter four games into his professional career and then started every game he played until his retirement in 1981. In Minnesota, he was part of one of the best defensive lines in NFL history, a fearsome group that became known as the "Purple People Eaters." Prior to Page joining the team, the Vikings had never won more than eight games in a season; during his tenure, Minnesota averaged 10 wins per year.

Even at his prime, though, Page was well aware he couldn't play the game forever. So he enrolled in law school at the University of Minnesota and earned his juris doctor in 1978. In the NFL off-season, he practiced employment law at a Minneapolis-based firm and eventually joined the staff of Minnesota's attorney general.

Page was reelected to Minnesota's Supreme Court in 1998, 2004, and 2010, stepping down from the bench in 2015 when he hit the state's 70-year-old retirement age for justices. IIn 2018, he was awarded the Presidential Medal of Freedom, as shown in this photo.

Position: **Defensive Tackle**

Hometown: **Canton, OH**

Born: **Aug. 7, 1945**

Height: **6'4"**

Weight: **245 lbs.**

Teams: **Minnesota Vikings (1967–78),
   Chicago Bears (1978–81)**

Career Sacks: **148.5**

Walter Payton

Walter Payton didn't immediately try out for football when he got to John J. Jefferson High School in Mississippi. His older brother Eddie was a star player, and Walter didn't want to compete against him. Instead, Walter ran track, played the drums in the marching band, and sang in the choir.

After Eddie graduated, though, the school's football coach approached the rising junior and asked him to join the team. Walter agreed, but only if he could keep playing in the marching band. The coach said okay and was immediately rewarded for his flexibility. On the very first carry in his high school career, the future Hall of Fame running back scampered 65 yards for a touchdown.

The youngest of Edward and Alyne Payton's three children, Walter was born in Columbia, Mississippi, on July 25, 1953. Though Walter had an excellent high school football career–scoring in every game he played–none of the top schools in the South offered him a scholarship. Such was life for many Black athletes when most southern schools were just starting to integrate.

Though he first committed to Kansas State University, he ultimately decided to enroll at Jackson State University, where his brother Eddie played football. It was there he earned the moniker "Sweetness," both for his graceful athleticism and good-natured personality. He was twice named the Black College Player of the Year, and he was a member of the 1974 College Football All-American team. No longer overlooked, Payton was chosen by the Chicago Bears as the fourth pick of the 1975 NFL draft.

He didn't exactly start his NFL career with a bang, netting zero yards on eight carries in his debut. That early humiliation fueled him, though, and he soon came to dominate. He made the Pro Bowl his second year and was league MVP the next season after rushing for 1,852 yards and 14 touchdowns. Though he wasn't the biggest back, he relished contact, often turning the tables on would-be tacklers by ducking his head and exploding into them.

In 1984, he broke Jim Brown's record of 12,312 career rushing yards. By the time he retired in 1987, Payton had extended his record to 16,726 yards. That number stood until Emmitt Smith surpassed it in 2002. While Payton was individually successful, the Bears struggled for a good portion of his early career. Things started to come together for the team in the early 1980s, and in 1985 Chicago finally broke through, going 15–1 in the regular season on the way to demolishing the Patriots 46–10 in the Super Bowl.

Payton rushed for over 1,000 yards in 10 of his 13 seasons, made the Pro Bowl nine times, and was a first-team All-Pro five times. Remarkably, he missed just one game his entire career– in his rookie season. Payton was inducted into the Hall of Fame in 1993.

Unfortunately, Sweetness died on November 1, 1999, at the age of 45 after being diagnosed with a rare liver disease called primary sclerosing cholangitis. The NFL honored Payton by renaming its Man of the Year community service award after him.

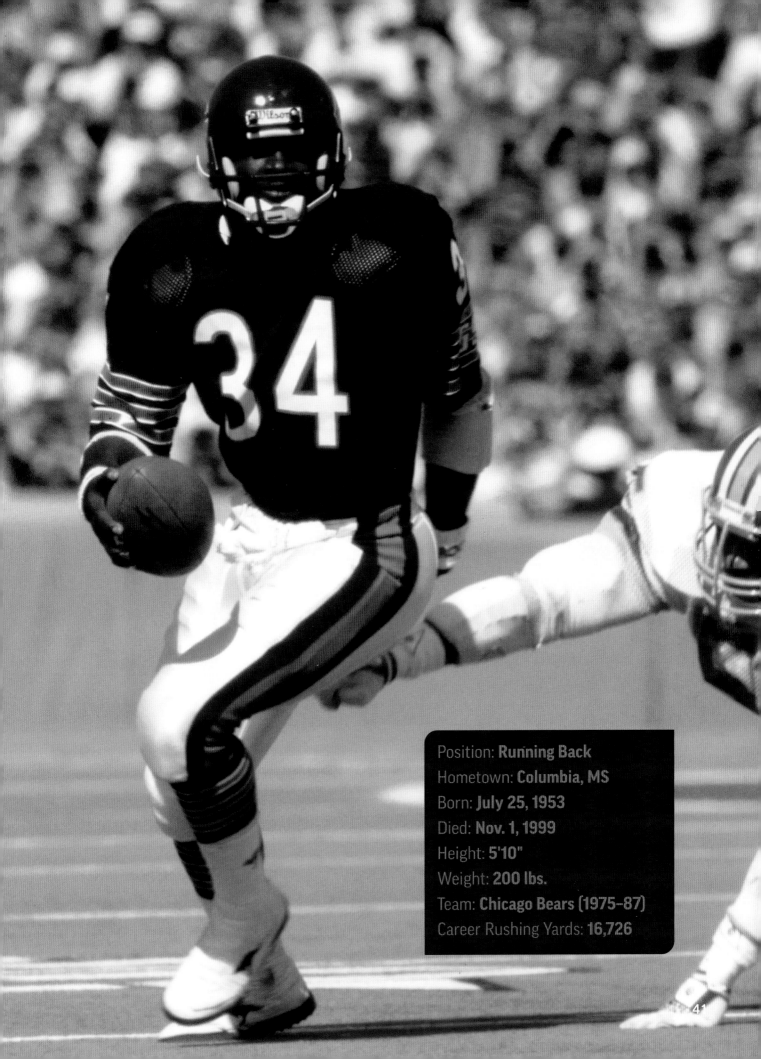

Position: **Running Back**
Hometown: **Columbia, MS**
Born: **July 25, 1953**
Died: **Nov. 1, 1999**
Height: **5'10"**
Weight: **200 lbs.**
Team: **Chicago Bears (1975–87)**
Career Rushing Yards: **16,726**

Troy Polamalu

Football was never a sport in the eyes of Hall of Fame safety Troy Polamalu. It was a spiritual battle. The deeply religious member of the Greek Orthodox Church spent much of his practices and games in intense prayer, so much so that coaches sometimes had difficulty getting his attention on the field.

"You've gotta pick and choose when you talk to Troy," said Bill Cowher, who was the head coach of the Pittsburgh Steelers during the first part of Polamalu's career. "You go up to him, and if he's got his head down, you have to wait and catch eye contact with him. That's the first step—you have to get his eyes before you get his ears."

Polamalu wasn't born into the Christian life. He entered the world on April 19, 1981, to a family falling apart. His father left shortly after Troy's birth, so it was up to his mom Suila to raise him and his four older siblings. Troy's brother was in and out of jail, and his three sisters had babies while in high school.

Troy said he spent the first nine years of his life as a "city rat," stealing lunch from a local grocery store on a daily basis and breaking into buildings. The trajectory of Troy's life changed, however, in the summer before fourth grade following a visit to his uncle's house in rural Oregon. Troy fell in love with Oregon's natural beauty and begged his mom to let him stay. He knew the type of life that awaited him back in California, and Troy yearned for something different. Reluctantly, Suila agreed.

The Polamalus are of American Samoan descent, and Troy's Uncle Salu adhered to the Samoan way centered on respect for family, church, and community. Troy found Salu's old-school discipline more of a relief than a burden.

Salu was the one who introduced Troy to organized sports, and at Douglas High School in Winston, Oregon, he excelled in football, basketball, and baseball. Another uncle, Kennedy Pola, was a former fullback at the University of Southern California, and he convinced then-coach Paul Hackett to look at Troy's film. Hackett offered Troy a spot on the team. Polamalu insists the match was divinely inspired. After all, his name is Troy, and USC's nickname is the Trojans.

At USC, Polamalu thrived both on and off the field. He was a consensus All-American in 2002, which was also the year he met his future wife Theodora Holmes. In the 2003 NFL draft, the Steelers traded up 11 spots to select Polamalu, who quickly became a fan favorite in Pittsburgh for his big plays and trademark long hair, which flowed out the back of his helmet.

Former teammate Chris Hope once said Polamalu played "like a controlled tornado." He helped the Steelers win two Super Bowls during his 12-year career. In the 2009 AFC Championship game, his late fourth-quarter pick-six against the Baltimore Ravens sealed Pittsburgh's trip to Super Bowl XLIII.

In his career, he was an eight-time Pro Bowler and a four-time first-team All-Pro. He was inducted into the Hall of Fame in 2020.

Position: **Safety**
Hometown: **Santa Ana, CA**
Born: **Apr. 19, 1981**
Height: **5'10"**
Weight: **207 lbs.**
Team: **Pittsburgh Steelers (2003–14)**
Career Interceptions: **32**

Jerry Rice

Jerry Rice had no desire to play football. And on one fateful day as a student at B. L. Moor High School in Crawford, Mississippi, he had no desire to attend class either, so he tried to sneak off campus. The assistant principal spotted him, and a chase ensued. Eventually, the assistant principal tracked Jerry down, but he was so impressed by the youngster's speed and elusiveness, he handed down a unique punishment: The boy had to start practicing with the football team.

Football owes a debt of gratitude for that educator's out-of-the-box thinking, for in the hierarchy of football greatness, there are stars, all-stars, and legends—and then there is Jerry Rice. In his 20-year NFL career, the wide receiver didn't just break records, he obliterated them, launching himself in a stratosphere of his very own.

Rice entered the league in 1985 as the San Francisco 49ers' first round draft choice out of unheralded Mississippi Valley State University. It took less than eight seasons for him to break Steve Largent's touchdown reception record by catching his 101st in 1992. He would finish his career with 197. A couple of years later, Rice passed Jim Brown to become the NFL's all-time touchdown leader with 127. He finished his career with 208. His 22,895 career receiving yards are over 5,000 more than any other player, and his 1,549 career receptions are over 100 more than the nearest competitor.

A skilled route-runner, Rice had the unique ability to cut explosively at full blast, putting even the best cornerbacks on their heels. He could also outjump defenders for balls, and his hands were incomparable. In college, he earned the nickname "World" because there was not a ball in the world Rice couldn't catch. "He can catch a BB on a dead run at night," Rice's college coach Archie Cooley said.

But Rice didn't rely on his physical gifts alone. He possessed an obsessive work ethic, meticulously cataloging the tendencies of defensive backs, following a strict healthy diet, and staying in peak condition by regularly sprinting across a long, steep hill in California's Edgewood County Park & Natural Preserve. His cooldown of 10 100-yard "easy stride-outs" up the hill was more intense than some of his peers' entire workouts.

Rice credited his father Joe Nathan for his relentless work ethic. Jerry was born October 13, 1962, in Crawford, Mississippi, and was one of eight children. Joe was a bricklayer, and in the hot and humid climate of the Deep South, he would have Jerry and his brothers assist him by tossing and catching bricks on a scaffold. The experience taught Jerry what hard work meant.

As he was coming out of college, not every team was sold on Rice considering the subpar competition he had faced. But San Francisco, fresh off a Super Bowl victory, wanted him and traded up in the first round to snag him. The addition of an all-world receiver to an already loaded lineup almost seemed unfair, and with Rice, the 49ers won three additional Super Bowls.

He finished his career in 2004 at the age of 42, having made 13 Pro Bowls and being named a first-team All-Pro 10 times. Jerry Rice joined the Hall of Fame in 2010.

Position: **Wide Receiver**
Hometown: **Crawford, MS**
Born: **Oct. 13, 1962**
Height: **6'2"**
Weight: **200 lbs.**
Teams: **San Francisco 49ers (1985–2000), Oakland Raiders (2001–4), Seattle Seahawks (2004)**
Career Receiving Touchdowns: **197**

Deion Sanders

After watching his friend Deion Sanders score 30 points in a high school basketball game, Richard Fain started calling him "Prime Time." And a better-fitting nickname there never was. Deion, who would go on to play both professional baseball and football, was brash, flamboyant, and larger-than-life. Either loved or hated–people couldn't take their eyes off him.

The future Hall of Fame cornerback was born August 9, 1967, in Fort Myers, Florida. His parents divorced when Deion was two, leaving his mother Connie Knight to raise him and his sister. Knight worked as a cook and a custodian at a local hospital to support her children, and Deion would internalize his mother's work ethic.

Knight signed her son up for sports early on to try to keep him occupied and out of trouble. By high school, it had become clear sports could be an avenue for much bigger things for him. At North Fort Myers High, Deion played baseball, basketball, and football–and was an all-state honoree in each. He opted to attend Florida State University on a football scholarship.

In college, Sanders once again competed in multiple sports. Aside from football, he played outfield for the baseball team and ran track. Though he helped Florida State win conference championships in each sport, he stood out most on the gridiron. He was a consensus All-American his junior and senior seasons and won the Jim Thorpe Award as the nation's top defensive back in 1988.

All the while, he remained Prime Time. He arrived for his final home game against rival Florida in a white limousine sporting a tuxedo.

At the 1989 NFL draft, Sanders wore thousands of dollars worth of gold jewelry as well as a leather ensemble with an embroidered "Prime Time."

The Atlanta Falcons selected Sanders with the fifth overall pick. The previous year, the New York Yankees had chosen him in the 30th round of MLB's draft. On September 5, 1989, he hit a home run against the Seattle Mariners. A few days later on the 10th, he made his NFL debut, returning a punt 68 yards for a touchdown. Before then, nobody had ever homered in an MLB game and scored an NFL touchdown in the same week.

Sanders continued splitting time between baseball and football for much of his career. In 1992, now with the Atlanta Braves, Sanders batted .533 in the World Series against the Toronto Blue Jays. A couple years later, following the 1994 NFL season, Sanders won the Super Bowl as a member of the San Francisco 49ers. He is the only person in history to play in both the World Series and the Super Bowl.

Though he was the NFL's Defensive Player of the Year in 1994, Sanders opted not to re-sign with San Francisco. Instead, he joined the Dallas Cowboys, where he won his second-straight Super Bowl.

Sanders retired after the 2000 season only to come back for two more years in 2004 and 2005. In all, he was an eight-time Pro Bowler and six-time first-team All-Pro. When he retired, his 19 career return touchdowns were an NFL record (since broken by Devin Hester). He was inducted into the Hall of Fame in 2011.

Position: **Cornerback**

Hometown: **Fort Myers, FL**

Born: **Aug. 9, 1967**

Height: **6'1"**

Weight: **195 lbs.**

Teams: **Atlanta Falcons (1989–93), San Francisco 49ers (1994), Dallas Cowboys (1995–99), Washington Redskins (2000), Baltimore Ravens (2004–5)**

Career Return Touchdowns: **19**

Bruce Smith

George Smith received an unexpected call on the day of his son's second high school football practice. The coach of Booker T. Washington High School in Norfolk, Virginia, wanted to know why George's son Bruce hadn't shown up.

Bruce's absence was news to George, who confronted his son about it. Bruce said football was "too hard, too hot, too painful." That invoked a look from George only a disapproving father can give. George asked Bruce if he thought George enjoyed getting up at sunrise each morning to go to work, not returning until sunset.

"Get back out there and show them what you're made of," George said. "Whatever you do in life, don't ever quit." Those words resonated with Bruce, no doubt in part because George walked the walk. He and his wife Annie worked long hours for minimum wage, but that didn't prevent them from being involved parents who filled their household with love and discipline.

That talk, in fact, became one of the defining moments of the future NFL Hall of Fame defensive end's life. "In that moment, I decided to commit myself to every endeavor," the longtime Buffalo Bill said. And, as it turned out, there was no stopping a fully committed Bruce Smith.

In high school, he excelled on the wrestling mat and the baseball diamond while also helping lead Booker T. to a state championship in basketball. He was an all-American football star as well, and football was where Bruce's future lay. He committed to play college ball at Virginia Tech, where after his senior year in 1984 he won the Outland Trophy, which is given to the nation's best interior lineman. Buffalo made him the first overall pick in the subsequent 1985 NFL draft.

After a mediocre rookie year that saw Smith record just 6.5 sacks while struggling to stay in shape, he once again decided to fully commit, this time to conditioning. He changed his diet and set out to become the best conditioned player in the league. He went from weighing over 300 pounds to a finely tuned 265 pounds, unlocking a combination of strength and speed that overwhelmed offensive linemen.

The new and improved Smith was, in a word, dominant. He finished with 15 sacks in 1986, and he had double-digit sacks every year after that through 1998 (except for 1991, when injuries limited him to five games). He finished his 19-year career with 11 Pro Bowls, eight first-team All-Pro selections, and was twice named the Defensive Player of the Year. He retired after the 2003 season having recorded an NFL record of 200 career sacks.

He was also an indispensable part of one of the most unique dynasties in all of professional sports. The Bills appeared in an unprecedented four-straight Super Bowls from 1991 to 1994, only to lose each and every one of them. Smith, though, has made peace with that legacy. "I think if you look at what we did, winning four AFC titles in a row when everyone else in the AFC desperately wanted to knock us off, that will stand the test of time," he said.

Position: **Defensive End**

Hometown: **Nor folk, VA**

Born: **June 18, 1963**

Height: **6'4"**

Weight: **262 lbs.**

Teams: **Buffalo Bills (1985–99),
    Washington Redskins
    (2000–2003)**

Career Sacks: **200**

Emmitt Smith

Emmitt James Smith III isn't particularly tall—he stands just 5'9". And he wasn't known for being especially fast—at least for a running back. But the NFL's all-time rushing leader had one out-of-this-world asset: his vision. He could anticipate how defenses would react and run toward openings that hadn't even materialized yet.

That prescience apparently didn't confine itself to the football field. At the age of six, he recalls watching a Dallas Cowboys game with some family members and turning to his father and saying, "One day I'm going to play professional football and I'm going to play for the Dallas Cowboys." Check and check.

Emmitt, the son of Emmitt Jr. and Mary, was born in Pensacola, Florida, on May 15, 1969. He and his parents, three brothers, and two sisters lived in a small apartment in a housing project. His father drove a city bus, and though money was tight, Emmitt never felt disadvantaged. More importantly, he experienced the love of his family each and every day.

He first began playing football at eight, and from a young age he knew two things: He wanted to be successful, and football was a way to achieve that success. He viewed it as a means to get an education, and by the time he was in high school, he had started to realize just how far football could take him.

Escambia High School had no history of gridiron success. Prior to 1982, the Gators hadn't had a winning season in nearly two decades. Then the Emmitt Smith era began. The phenom led Escambia to back-to-back state championships his sophomore and junior years, and *Parade* magazine named Smith its High School Player of the Year following his senior season.

Just about every college football program in the country vied for Smith's attention, but he decided to remain in state—and remain a Gator—by choosing to play at the University of Florida. In just three college seasons, he broke 58 school records, including career rushing yards (3,928), rushing touchdowns (37), and yards per game (126.7).

He declared for the 1990 NFL draft, and the prophecy he made as a six-year-old came true when the Dallas Cowboys selected him with the 17th overall pick. In Dallas, Smith teamed up with quarterback Troy Aikman and wide receiver Michael Irvin. Known as the "Triplets," the trio helped the Cowboys become a dynasty in the mid-1990s, winning three Super Bowls between the 1992 and 1995 seasons. Smith was a first-team All-Pro each of those four years, and he made the Pro Bowl in each of his first six years in the league.

His career culminated on October 22, 2002, when he broke Walter Payton's all-time NFL rushing yards record, surpassing Payton's 16,726-yard mark. He finished his career with 18,355 rushing yards as well as 164 rushing touchdowns, also an NFL record.

Smith retired in 2004 and gained further fame in 2006 when he won the third season of ABC's *Dancing with the Stars*. He was inducted in the Pro Football Hall of Fame in 2010.

Position: **Running Back**
Hometown: **Pensacola, FL**
Born: **May 15, 1969**
Height: **5'9"**
Weight: **221 lbs.**
Teams: **Dallas Cowboys (1990–2002),**
  Arizona Cardinals (2003–4)
Career Rushing Yards: **18,355**

Lawrence Taylor

Lawrence Taylor had amazing grit. The New York Giants' legendary outside linebacker entered an important game against the New Orleans Saints on November 27, 1988, with torn shoulder ligaments and a detached pectoral muscle. To keep his shoulder in place, he had to wear a harness. But what would have kept mere mortals from suiting up didn't slow Taylor down—not even a little. He recorded three sacks while forcing two fumbles, and New York squeaked out a 13–12 victory.

Giants head coach Bill Parcells called Taylor's performance the greatest game he ever saw. Taylor, who could convince himself of nearly anything, once said playing through pain was merely a matter of tricking yourself into thinking you aren't hurt.

Taylor's approach to his position combined with his out-of-this-world athleticism revolutionized football. Before Taylor, the outside linebacker was essentially a "read and react" position. Taylor changed it into an attacking, aggressive one. No running back stood a chance blocking him at 6'3" and 237 pounds. And yet he was also much too fast for most offensive linemen to handle.

"He changed the way defense is played, the way pass-rushing is played, the way linebackers play, and the way offenses block linebackers," Hall of Fame player, coach, and broadcaster John Madden said. Taylor didn't just transform the linebacker position, his existence changed the offensive line as well. Size and strength were no longer sufficient. Linemen—especially offensive tackles—now also had to be nimble and quick-footed.

Lawrence Taylor was born on February 4, 1959, in Williamsburg, Virginia. His father Clarence worked in the shipyards in Newport News, Virginia, while his mother Iris worked odd jobs to earn the family some extra money. Lawrence could be a handful as a child. Where his two brothers would ask permission to do things, Lawrence approached life with more of a "shoot first, ask questions later" philosophy.

He grew up playing baseball and singing in his church's choir and didn't play football until his junior year at Lafayette High School. He quickly became a star and accepted a football scholarship at the University of North Carolina. Respect was important to Taylor, and he first tried to get it by picking fights all over Chapel Hill. Eventually he learned a better way was through total domination on the football field.

During his senior year, Taylor set a program record with 16 sacks on his way to being an All-American. In a poll prior to the 1981 NFL draft, 26 of the league's 28 general managers said they would draft Taylor No. 1. One of the two teams that did not name Taylor, New Orleans, actually owned that top spot and drafted running back George Rogers. That freed the Giants to pick up Taylor.

Taylor exploded onto the scene and was named the league's Defensive Player of the Year as a rookie. In 1986, after recording 20.5 sacks, Taylor became just the second defensive player to win the NFL's Most Valuable Player Award. He made the Pro Bowl in each of his first 10 seasons and was an eight-time first-team All-Pro selection. During his 13-year career, Taylor led the Giants to Super Bowl victories in 1987 and 1991. He was elected into the Hall of Fame in 1999.

Position: **Linebacker**
Hometown: **Williamsburg, VA**
Born: **Feb. 4, 1959**
Height: **6'3"**
Weight: **237 lbs.**
Team: **New York Giants (1981–93)**
Career Sacks: **142**

Johnny Unitas

The greatest quarterback of his generation began his professional football career earning six dollars per game for the semiprofessional Bloomfield Rams. Johnny Unitas was not considered a top prospect heading into the 1955 NFL draft. Many scouts doubted the University of Louisville product had the size, at 6'1" and weighing about 170 pounds, to compete at football's highest level.

But it wasn't Unitas's size that doomed him that year. It was his perceived lack of intelligence. The Pittsburgh Steelers drafted Unitas in the ninth round over the objections of head coach Walt Kiesling, who did not think Unitas was smart enough to run an NFL offense. Kiesling cut the rookie prior to the start of the season. Unitas didn't even appear in a single preseason game.

That wasn't the first time he had been underestimated. Born on May 7, 1933, to Leon and Helen Unitas, John Constantine Unitas was the third of four children, raised in the working-class section of Pittsburgh. Leon owned a small coal delivery business before he died of pneumonia when Johnny was just five years old. Helen picked up the slack, going to night school to become a bookkeeper in order to provide for her family. Later, Johnny would say he learned more about courage from his mother than from any coach.

Johnny became the starting quarterback at St. Justin's High School his junior year, and he was named to the All-Catholic High School team as a senior. His dream was to play at Notre Dame, but the Irish coaching staff considered him too small at about 145 pounds. The University of Pittsburgh offered him a scholarship, but Unitas couldn't pass the school's entrance exams.

The University of Louisville threw Unitas a lifeline, which he took. The Cardinals were not part of the NCAA at the time and so were not very well-regarded. Nevertheless, Unitas had some individual success, though injuries and subpar teams kept him flying under the radar.

Things turned around in 1956 when Unitas played well enough for the Bloomfield Rams that the Baltimore (now Indianapolis) Colts offered him a tryout and ended up signing him to back up starter George Shaw. Then as fate would have it, Shaw injured himself in the fourth game of the '56 season, opening the door for Unitas.

In 1957, he led the league in passing yards (2,550) and touchdown passes (24), and in 1958 he quarterbacked the Colts to an NFL championship. The '58 title game against the New York Giants was dubbed "the greatest football game ever played," helping boost the sport's popularity nationwide. The Colts won the championship again the next year, and Unitas also helped Baltimore win Super Bowl V in 1971.

In his 18-year career, Unitas made 10 Pro Bowls and was a first-team All-Pro five times. He was the first quarterback to throw for over 40,000 career yards, and he once threw a touchdown in 47 straight games, a record that stood until 2012. He was inducted into the Hall of Fame in 1979.

Unitas, the Hall of Famer once considered too small—both in mind and stature—for professional football, passed away September 11, 2002. He suffered a heart attack while working out at age 69.

Position: **Quarterback**
Hometown: **Pittsburgh, PA**
Born: **May 7, 1933**
Died: **Sept. 11, 2002**
Height: **6'1"**
Weight: **194 lbs.**
Teams: **Baltimore Colts (1956–72),**
San Diego Chargers (1973)
Career Passing Yards: **40,239**

Adam Vinatieri

The legend Tom Brady, winner of an NFL record seven Super Bowls, might never have gotten off the ground if it weren't first for another legend: an undrafted field goal kicker from South Dakota.

In the 2002 divisional round of the playoffs, the New England Patriots found themselves trailing the Oakland Raiders 13–10. With under a minute to play and no time-outs left, New England trotted Adam Vinatieri out to attempt a 45-yard field goal in blizzard-like conditions. Tromping through four to five inches of snow, Vinatieri kicked the ball through the uprights, keeping the Patriots' season alive. Some consider it the greatest field goal ever made.

Adam Vinatieri made another, much shorter, field goal in overtime, sending New England to the AFC championship game, where they beat the Pittsburgh Steelers to advance to Super Bowl XXXVI. There, against the vaunted St. Louis Rams, he kicked a 48-yarder in a tied game as time expired, giving Brady and the Patriots franchise their first Super Bowl title.

Vinatieri was born in the small town of Yankton, South Dakota. Shortly afterward, his father's military career took the Vinatieris to Germany for a couple of years before they settled in Rapid City, South Dakota. The second oldest of four children, Adam spent much of his childhood trying to catch up with his older brother Chad. The sibling rivalry fostered a competitive spirit in Adam, and he would need every bit of it to survive his childhood.

While in elementary school, Adam was diagnosed with a learning disability that made it difficult for him to read and spell. He spent time in special education classes, which wreaked havoc on the young boy's self-esteem. But those classes were led by an exceptional teacher named Marcy Farrand, who gave Adam the confidence to overcome his struggles. Adam doubled his efforts and eventually became an honor student at Rapid City's Central High School.

Vinatieri wound up kicking for South Dakota State University, at the time an NCAA Division II school. He had a good if not stellar college career, but no NFL teams came calling and he spent a year kicking for the Amsterdam Admirals of the World League of American Football before the Patriots signed him as an undrafted free agent in 1996.

With New England, Vinatieri won a total of three Super Bowls. In Super Bowl XXXVIII, history repeated itself when Vinatieri yet again nailed a game-winner in the final seconds against the Carolina Panthers, cementing himself as the greatest clutch kicker in history. After the 2005 season, he joined the Indianapolis Colts, where he won a fourth ring in the 2007 Super Bowl.

During his 24-year career that ended in 2019, Vinatieri made an NFL-record 599 field goals, and nobody in league history has scored more points than his 2,673. He made 29 game-winning kicks, was named to three Pro Bowls, and was a first-team All-Pro selection three times.

Position: **Kicker**

Hometown: **Yankton, SD**

Born: **Dec. 28, 1972**

Height: **6'**

Weight: **212 lbs.**

Teams: **New England Patriots (1996–2005), Indianapolis Colts (2006–19)**

Career Field Goal Percentage: **83.8%**

Reggie White

At the age of 12, Reginald Howard White told his mother he had two life goals: play professional football and become a minister. He checked off one when he was ordained a Baptist minister at 17. By then, the high school All-American football star was also well on his way to accomplishing the other too.

Reggie was born on December 19, 1961, in Chattanooga, Tennessee. His mom Thelma Collier raised him until he turned eight, when he went to live with his grandmother Mildred Dodd. The player later credited Dodd for his faith. She would often walk to church several miles away, and her steadfast commitment made an impression on the boy.

Meanwhile, on the football field, Reggie was the one making impressions. As a senior at Howard High School, the 6'5" defensive lineman was terrorizing opponent backfields, recording 10 sacks and 140 combined tackles. He was considered the best prospect in Tennessee and decided to stay in state at the University of Tennessee.

In his final year as a Volunteer, the so-called "Minister of Defense" proved to be one of the nation's premier players. He had a school record 15 sacks on his way to being a consensus All-American and Southeastern Conference Player of the Year. Though in high demand among many NFL teams, White, enticed by the idea of staying close to home, decided to sign with the Memphis Showboats of the United States Football League.

After his second year, though, the USFL folded. The Philadelphia Eagles took White with the fourth pick of the 1984 NFL supplemental draft, and he made an impact immediately in a home game on September 29, 1985, against the New York Giants. In his NFL debut, White sacked Giants quarterback Phil Simms 2.5 times and deflected a pass the Eagles then intercepted and returned for a touchdown. By the fourth quarter, the ecstatic crowd was chanting, "Reg-gie! Reg-gie!"

White quickly cemented himself as the most dominant defender in the NFL. Beginning in 1986, he made an unprecedented 13 straight Pro Bowls while being named a first-team All-Pro eight times. "Reggie changed offenses," said former Giants linebacker Mike Whittington. "Whatever they had planned was based upon his existence."

White changed more than offensive game plans, though—he changed the entire league. In 1992 he was among a handful of players who sued the NFL for more player choice around free agency. At the time, players basically could only become free agents if the team that drafted them didn't want them anymore. Because of the lawsuit, players won the right to sign with any team once their contract expired.

In 1993, White became an unrestricted free agent and surprised everyone by signing with the Green Bay Packers. The move paid off when the Packers made it to back-to-back Super Bowls in 1997 and 1998, beating the New England Patriots in '97. White retired following the 1998 season but came back in 2000 before retiring for good after one season with the Carolina Panthers. His 198 career sacks were a league record.

White died unexpectedly on December 26, 2004, from a fatal cardiac arrhythmia. He left behind his wife Sara and children Jeremy and Jecolia. He was inducted posthumously into the Hall of Fame in 2006.

Position: **Defensive End**

Hometown: **Chattanooga, TN**

Born: **Dec. 19, 1961**

Died: **Dec. 26, 2004**

Height: **6'5"**

Weight: **291 lbs.**

Teams: **Philadelphia Eagles (1985–92),
    Green Bay Packers (1993–98),
    Carolina Panthers (2000)**

Career Sacks: **198**

Kellen Winslow

Cornelius Perry badly wanted Kellen Winslow on his team. The football coach at East St. Louis High School in Illinois had noticed the freshman's athletic gifts in gym class and recognized a special talent when he saw it. There was just one problem: Kellen had absolutely no interest in football.

Kellen's passion lay not on a playing field but on a chessboard. He was in a chess club and played the game whenever he got a chance. He and his group of friends loved the game so much, they wore T-shirts imprinted with "Chess Nuts."

But Perry was relentless. "You belong on a football field whether you know it or not," the coach once told the youngster. Finally, after three years of begging, Perry's persistence paid off, and Kellen agreed to strap on the pads his senior year. He immediately became the team's starting tight end.

Kellen was one of seven children. His father was a bus driver, and his mother was a clerical assistant for several offices. The family did not have a lot of money, and from a young age Kellen planned on earning a scholarship in order to attend college. He had just assumed that scholarship would be an academic one. But during his lone year of high school football, Kellen's size—he stood 6'4" at the time—and athleticism attracted college scouts, and he ended up accepting a football scholarship at the University of Missouri.

New to the game, Winslow applied his knowledge of chess to the gridiron. During his sophomore year of college, he had a minor epiphany: He was like the knight on a chessboard. Once he started looking at it in those terms, football began to make more sense, as he was able to understand how all of the different positions on the field fit together to accomplish a common goal.

By his senior year at Missouri, Winslow had grown to 6'5" and weighed 250 pounds. NFL scouts were intrigued by how fast and fluid a man of his size was. In the 1979 draft, the San Diego Chargers traded up to select Winslow with the 13th pick. However, it took the Chargers and their visionary coach Don Coryell a little while to fully comprehend what they had in Winslow.

In those days, tight ends primarily served as extra blockers and outlet receivers. And that's how San Diego used Winslow during his rookie year. But blocking wasn't Winslow's strength, and he only caught 25 passes for 255 yards and two touchdowns that season. In the offseason, offensive coordinator Joe Gibbs had the idea of aligning Winslow all over the field to create favorable matchups and take advantage of his unique athleticism.

The plan worked. In 1980 and 1981, Winslow led the NFL in receptions. He made the Pro Bowl each year from 1980 through 1983, and he was a first-team All-Pro from 1980 through 1982. In the process, Winslow revolutionized the tight end position.

Winslow's career was cut short due to knee injuries, forcing him to retire following the 1987 season at the age of 30. Still, he finished with a total of 541 receptions for 6,741 yards and was inducted into the Hall of Fame in 1995.

Position: **Tight End**
Hometown: **St. Louis, MO**
Born: **Nov. 5, 1957**
Height: **6'5"**
Weight: **251 lbs.**
Team: **San Diego Chargers (1979–87)**
Career Receptions: **541**

August 29, 2015: Quarterback Peyton Manning
(far right) of the Denver Broncos gets ready
to throw a pass during a game against the
San Francisco 49ers.